ANCIENT ROME

THE RISE AND FALL OF AN EMPIRE

THE HISTORY HOUR

HISTORY

CONTENTS

❧ I ❦

INTRODUCTION

Rome has grown since its humble beginnings that it is now overwhelmed by its own greatness.
  Titus Livius

❦❧❦

A boy named Romulus was the first ruler of Rome. A boy named Romulus was its last ruler. It is said that such is the stuff of tales and legends. Yet the crumpled ruins of columns, arches and cobblestone streets scattered over three continents stand as silent sentinels to the naked reality that once was Rome.

❦❧❦

This history of the Ancient Roman World utilizes the records of ancient historians, poets and contemporary scholars as well. It presents fascinating myths, legends and prophecies. In addition, included are pertinent facts, dates, traditions and descriptions about the myriad of cultures within the borders of the Ancient Roman Empire. The structure and organization of the Roman Republic and the Roman Empire are also discussed, as well as the accomplishments and failure of the Roman Emperors. The information imparted inside is based on documented sources and encompasses:

෴

- The Code of Roman Law
- Evolving Organizational Structure
- True stories of the Roman citizens– both the humble and the haughty
- Assassinations and Conspiracies
- Battles and Wars
- Emperors and Military Commanders
- Goals and motivations of the Roman leadership
- Causes and Effects of the Rise and Fall of Ancient Rome
- The Barbaric Invasions

II

ANCIENT ROME – A MYTH EVOLVES INTO AN EMPIRE

If you have overcome your inclination and not been overcome by it, you have reason to rejoice.

Plautus

753 BC – 44 BC FROM FRATRICIDE
TO ASSASSINATION

❧

"Rise up my Avenging Spirit"
The Tragic Myth

❧

According to Virgil, the Roman poet who lived during the 1st Century BC, the sailor, Aeneas, escaped war-torn Troy (in current-day Turkey) during the 8th Century BC. He sailed to Rome after stopping at Carthage in North Africa. Although there is no archeological evidence of the ancient city of Troy, it is highlighted in the works of Homer's *Iliad* and *Odyssey* and Virgil epic tale, the *Aeneid*.

❧

According to Virgil, Aeneas met Dido, the Phoenician Queen of Carthage. They had a love affair and married. Having had a vision from the god Mercury that Carthage was not the haven he craved, Aeneas felt obliged to leave her. After Aeneas left, Queen Dido – grief-stricken and despondent – committed suicide by heaving her body upon a burning funeral pyre. As she was dying, she screamed,

"Rise up my bones, my avenging spirit!"

⚶

As Virgil tells it, Aeneas fulfilled his destiny and was an ancestor to Romulus and Remus. Because they were born of a vestal virgin and they were supposed to be sentenced to death. However, a kindly servant placed the twins in a basket and sent them down the River Tiber. A she-wolf found the boys, suckled them. When a local Latin King found them he took them under his care, but the more aggressive twin, Romulus, slayed the King during an argument. Afterwards, they wandered until they spotted an area surrounded by seven hills. The two boys quarreled about which hill to choose for their new city but the dispute accelerated into combat and Romulus killed his brother. Romulus then chose Palatine Hill and named his city **"Rome"** after himself. Romulus allied himself with the Latin tribes in the area. As more people emigrated there, he intermingled with the Latin population.

⚶

Rome was ruled by a succession of seven kings. A man by the name of Lucumo from Greece reportedly became the second King there. The Latins were innovative people. The land was reportedly swampy, but they drained it and cleared the heavy forestation so as to erect dwellings and temples to their gods. The last king of early Rome was "Tarquin the Proud" who was a veritable tyrant, and was exiled by the outraged citizens.

6

※

THE ORACLE OF DELPHI

※

The people during this era were superstitious. Greeks, Romans, Latins and the Etruscans all had their own spiritual beliefs wrapped in the fear of displeasing the gods of the earth and sky. Among the specters they feared were were-wolves, lamias (horned and large-toothed creatures from the earth), vampires, ghosts and witches. To protect themselves from calamity, people wore amulets and consulted sooth-sayers (prophets and prophetesses). The soothsayers of the day read the future and warned them of pending disasters so they could protect themselves. One such prophetess was the Oracle of Delphi. She would lapse into a trance and utter her predictions. Earlier in this century, evidence was uncovered by archeologists that proved ethylene gas emerges from the trapped waters of an underground spring in Delphi. Ethylene vapors would be sufficient to induce a state of delirium. The tunneled route of this underground spring leads deep within the earth and pours into a warm dank pool deep within the volcanic rock. Hence, there may very well be some truth to the Oracle's existence. Each oracle had successors.

THE EARLY ETRUSCANS (ALSO KNOWN AS THE TYRRHENIANS)

࿓

North and Northwest of the Latin states lay an area known as Etruria. It was settled by the Etruscan tribes. They were traders, artisans and seamen. The Etruscans built their own fine wooden ships with two square sails and plied the waters of the Mediterranean Sea. Many were pirates – highly skilled and immensely powerful. In speaking of a merchant's capture of an Etruscan, Homer wrote in his epic, *Hymn to Dionysus*:

> "Madmen! What god is this whom you have taken and bound, strong that he is? ...Surely this is either Zeus or Apollo, who has the silver bow, or Poseidon, for he looks not like mortal men but like the gods who dwell on Olympus."

The Etruscans were virile, tall and incredibly masculine.

࿓

There were many artisans among the Etruscans. The famous sculpture *Capitoline Wolf* showing Romulus and Remus is made of Etruscan bronze. The Etruscan merchants traded their wares with Cyprus, Greece, Carthage and even Egypt. The goods were carried in beautiful amphorae, which were two-handled terracotta jugs of various shapes and sizes. Oil, olives, pottery, ingots, silver, bronze, grain and jewels were among the items that were traded. By the 6th Century BC, Etruria had expanded and its people were considered masters of the sea.

THE ROMAN REPUBLIC

❧

After the ruthless king, Tarquin the Proud, was expelled, the Romans set up a highly organized government. In the year 450 BC, they codified the *Twelve Tables*, which was the basis of Roman Law. For their leadership, they elected consuls and created a hierarchical set of elected officials, called magistrates, who served under them.

❧

The chief governing advisory body was the Roman Senate. It was composed of patricians (see below). Consuls were required to confer with them. Maintaining the separation of powers between the consuls and Senate was often difficult.

❧

In addition, Rome built up an army of highly disciplined

warriors. These fighters were heavily armored, carried spears, wore helmets called **"Galea"** and carried grand shields embossed with symbols of the Republic. They also built vessels propelled by series of rowers. The flagship and smaller ships had one or two sails. Vessels were basically four sizes based on the number and banks of rowers:

- **Tireme** – three banks of rowers stacked one above the other
- **Quinquerme** – three banks of rowers with two rowers per oar on the top two banks
- **Quadriremes** – two banks of rowers and space for marine fighters with one mast and sail
- **Hexareme** – three banks of rowers with two rowers on each bank

჻

The sturdiest of the ships had a *corvus*, which was a bridge that could be lowered on to the deck of an enemy vessel, permitting marines and seamen to board an enemy vessel and engage in hand-to-hand combat.

჻

The Roman shipbuilders used pitch to **"glue"** the wooden planks together that formed the hull of the ship. Pitch was readily available around Rome, as it could be produced from peat and organic matter from rotted crops. In ancient times, everything was organic!

THE PATRICIANS, PLEBEIANS
AND THE SLAVES

❧

S ociety was divided into three segments: the *plebeians,*
the patricians and the slaves. The patricians were the
government officials and those who owned and
managed the lands. The plebeians were the farmers and work-
ers. The slaves were prisoners of war and their families.

❧

THE PATRICIANS

❧

The patricians were members of the noble class. They were
educated and filled posts in the government. Many were the
descendants and favorites of the kings. In time, they became
wealthy from the cultivation of lands they owned. Patricians
employed plebeians to work the farms and sell the produce

at the many markets that were built in Rome and the environs.

⚜

Flat bronze was used as legal tender in the very beginning. (4th Century BC) A simple system of weights and measurements was used to determine the basis for exchange. Coins were cast in the 3rd Century BC and initially also made of bronze and later of silver and gold. The craftsmen embossed them with the profiles of their consuls and emperors.

⚜

Some of the patricians were sly and frequently cheated the plebeians or confiscated their goods and farm equipment. When they lent money to foreign traders, many patricians engaged in usury which made them even more wealthy. Unscrupulous magistrates raped the purses of the common people by convincing the Senate to pass levies and taxes. Senators were also guilty of that and some became enormously rich. When gold was introduced, the more conceited of the patricians used gold drinking chalices and plates. They also employed some of artisans to create elaborate mosaics to decorate their home. Senators wore gold rings and jewelry. Some had homes with running water, baths and even sewage systems.

⚜

In order to prevent influence and political interference from plebeians, the patricians forbade a plebeian to marry a patrician. They also denied plebeians the right to hold public office. That maintained their elite status.

※

This changed significantly in time.

※

THE PLEBEIANS

※

In prehistoric times, there was a massive volcano near Rome. Volcanic soil is extremely fertile and rich in minerals – excellent for the growing of crops. Corn grew easily and the plebeian framers planted orchards of olive trees. Olives were not only used for eating, but they were pressed and yielded olive oil for heating and cooking. Rome also sold olive oil to Greece and other areas around the Mediterranean.

※

Grasses readily grew on the hills around Rome, and the people raised cattle on those lands. Most of the lands around Rome were **"common lands,"** intended for farming and cattle grazing.

※

Towns grew up in the Roman territory. They housed many craftsmen who built the ships, created the amphora to carry goods across the sea and plied the iron from the bogs into armor. Shields were made of wood and leather.

The craftsmen also created household items including statues of the gods. (Every home had one.)

Some plebeians were pressed into military service, especially during times of war. When too many of their sons were forced to serve in the army, the traumatized families were devastated by the loss. This resulted in fields lying fallow, bleached by the sun or eroded by the rain and wind. Famine and disease followed.

Initially the plebeians weren't allowed to participate in government and couldn't vote. The plebeians rebelled against this in the 4th Century BC. They – the **"breadwinners"** of society - threatened to leave Rome. That terrified the patricians and concessions were made. Protests and two very clever secessions from the city occurred on occasions when abuses became extreme. On the first occasion, the plebeians actually departed the Seven Hills and relocated to Janiculum, which is outside the central city perimeter. That was enough to cause a reaction.

The *Plebeian Curiate Assembly* was then developed to protect their rights and meet their needs. Plebeian representatives called *Plebeian tribunes* were elected from among them. This assembly was a legislative body for the plebeians. In time, that evolved into a more representative body in the Roman Republic.

THE SLAVES

৩১৫

Slavery prevailed during the ancient Roman era. These people were those who had been conquered as result of war, and foreigners who entered the city without proper permissions. In the early years, they had no rights and were subjected to cruel punishments and torture. Female slaves were usually prostitutes. When more learned people became enslaved, fair-minded religious and political leaders granted them more rights, even the ownership of property from which they could sell crops and wares or become tutors. In time, they were permitted to buy their freedom and became Roman citizens. Even so, by the time they could afford that, they were usually old and infirm.

LEX VALERIAN – LEGAL RIGHTS
FOR THE PLEBEIANS

A s early as 509 BC, Publius Valerius Publicola, a
consul in the Roman government, recognized the
plight of the besieged plebeians who were so often
abused. Sometimes hard-working plebeians were scourged,
whipped or crucified because the patricians who employed
them felt they weren't performing up to expectations. The
Lex (or "law") gave the plebeians the right to appeal their
cases and deny the magistrates the right to execute or other-
wise torture them. However, edicts issued by the *Plebeian
Assembly* were only binding if they were ratified by the Senate.

THE REIGN OF TERROR

❈

During the consulship of Appius Claudius Crassus in the 5th Century BC, Appius and some of the patricians made a brash move and tried to subvert the *Twelve Tablets*. Appius and his conspirators then instigated a reign of terror and tyranny. As result, the plebeians utilized the power of the people and seceded again. This time, they went to another city – Aventine.

❈

With regard to the secession, the ancient historian, Livy, wrote that the kindly patricians, Valerius and Horatius, chided the Senate crying out

> "Are you going to administer justice to the walls and roofs? ...
> What if the plebeians come against us with arms?"

The Senate then sent messengers out to the plebeians to

negotiate a settlement. That culminated in a new law called the *Lex Valeri-Horatio*. (see below)

❦

THE HONOR KILLING

❦

Besides the gross aberration of the plebeian rights, Consul Appius committed other heinous crimes. This consul was a man ruled by his own desires. One time, he kidnapped a beautiful woman by the name of Verginia because he desired her. Appius then insisted that she was a slave girl, which wasn't true. Unfortunately, it resulted in an honor killing at that hands of her father who didn't want her violated by the evil consul.

❦

The Senate called a court session. They demanded that Appius step down and go into permanent exile for attempting to rewrite the laws and for the kidnapping. Rather than face his accusers, the cowardly consul committed suicide. Valerius (Valerius Potitus) and Horatius (Horatius Barbatus) were then elected the next consuls of the Roman Republic. Both social classes supported the two consuls wholeheartedly.

❦

෯෧

This law virtually eliminated the constant and persistent political power struggle between the plebeians and the patricians. Responsibilities shifted and the plebeian tribunes could have grievances heard before the Senate. In addition, laws passed by the plebeian assemblies were binding on *all* Roman citizens – patricians and plebeians alike. A series of checks and balances were employed to equalize the rights of both classes including voting. Various measures were taken to prevent Senatorial obstruction if some of the nobles or Senators tried to prevent or reduce the rights of the plebeians as Roman citizens.

෯෧

Although there was barbarity in Ancient Rome, there was justice, intelligence and understanding.

WAR WITH THE ETRUSCANS

The Roman territory expanded as the population did, and intruded on Etruria, which lay just North-West of Rome. By the 5th Century BC, Etruria had expanded North even into the Po Valley. Rome wanted those lands, as well as the cessation of skirmishes at the borders.

To organize and direct their armies, the Romans elected *Military tribunes* during times of war. In time, they had consular powers. Many of the military tribunes were plebeians. When Rome became desperate, they sporadically appointed dictators in order to bypass the usual legislative processes, which could be time-consuming.

Wars raged between Rome and Etruria on and off from 483 BC to 396 BC.

❦

THE BATTLES AT VEII

❦

The Roman soldiers encountered the Etruscans North of Veii. During the first phase of the battles, the Romans were brutally slaughtered and forced to retreat to the hills and shaded forests. After setting up new battlefield formations, they descended in vast numbers upon the people in Veii.

❦

Because Veii was the main city in Southern Etruria, it was a hub of commerce. There was a temple to the goddess Juno in the city center that also served as a fortress. Before the second phase of the battles, the Romans had a seaman consult the Oracle at Delphi regarding a suggestion one of the older townsmen had made. He proposed that a grand tunnel be built under the city and into the temple. The Oracle predicted that the tunnel would bring them victory, so they secretly dug it during the night.

❦

At daybreak, the Roman forces surrounded the city walls in order to lure the sequestered Etruscans out of the temple. After the Etruscans rushed out to defend the city's walls, the

Romans crawled into the temple via the tunnel. From there they attacked the Etruscans out in the open. Thousands of Etruscans were killed or captured. The males were viciously slaughtered and the women and children were forced into slavery.

WAR WITH THE GAUL

❦

In the 5th Century BC, Gaul (current-day France) was settled by Celtic tribes. During the following century, the Gallic tribes then migrated into Italy. They were on the rampage throughout the cities of Etruria that were still under the governance of the Etruscans. Although it seems very curious, the Etruscans asked Rome for assistance against these Gallic intruders when they threatened the city of Clusium. (located in Tuscany)

❦

THE MURDER AT CLUSIUM

❦

Upon the arrival of the Roman ambassador, Quintus Fabius, the people of Clusium asked him to intercede with the Gauls and come to a peace agreement. Fabius then met with the Gauls. Rather than conduct a negotiation, the impetuous Fabius thrust his sword into the body of a Gallic chief, slaying him. Brennus, the Gallic commander, was enraged. He and the Gauls then resolutely marched toward Rome, intent upon avenging the senseless murder. Gaul then declared war on Rome.

⚜

THE BATTLE OF THE ALLIA AND TIBER RIVER

⚜

The battleground for this engagement was straddled between two rivers – the Tiber and the Allia. The ferocious Gauls, accustomed to warfare, descended upon Rome. Historians differ significantly as to the number of soldiers involved in this tremendous battle, but it's clear from most records that the Romans made the inauspicious choice of using many poorly trained warriors.

⚜

> *"Rome was thunderstruck by the swiftness at which they moved," said Livy, "...as if it was meeting a spur-of-the-moment emergency."*

Observing that the Romans had a reserve unit holding back at a distance, Brennus, the Gallic commander, surprised them by attacking this unit first. Then Brennus turned to the main line of Roman soldiers. The Roman line was very thin at the center – a very unwise configuration. The Gauls made a frontal assault on the center of the line. Seeing that their force had been split in two, the Romans panicked and fled.

❦

Then Gauls then sacked Rome, destroying every building they could and setting fire to the wooden houses, shops and buildings. The dead and dying were left to bleed out on to the cobblestones of the markets and streets. It was a bloodbath. Gaul now occupied the city. However, upon Capitoline Hill was the magnificent temple and fortress dedicated to the goddess Juno that hadn't yet been attacked. Inside the temple, there was a defensive Roman force. They were too far from the raging battle in Rome and didn't hear it.

❦

GEESE SAVE THE TEMPLE!

❦

The defending Roman legion inside the Temple of Juno on Capitoline Hill were sleeping. This temple had a resident flock of geese which the people loved. When the Gallic tribal warriors ascended toward the temple *en masse*, the alarmed geese flew up and into the faces of the Gallic soldiers from all directions. This alarum awakened the sleeping Romans who counterattacked from the walls. The Gauls then abandoned their attack on the temple and retreated back to the city of Rome. Although the city was devastated, the temple was saved.

Polybius, another ancient historian, summarized the outcome of the Gallic conflict:

> "...after remaining masters of the city itself for seven months, (the Gauls) finally gave it up of their own free will and, as an act of grace, returned home with their spoils, unbroken and unscathed."

THE PUNIC WARS – 264 BC TO 146 BC

❧

"**P**unic" is from the Latin word "Punicus" meaning "Phoenician." The Phoenicians established the city of Carthage under the rulership of Queen Dido from Phoenicia (current-day Lebanon). She is the woman who met up with Aeneas as related in the beginning of this Chapter. The Phoenician city of Carthage is on the North African coast and lies along the Central Mediterranean Sea. Carthage was one of the major trading ports at that time. The Phoenicians were noted for being the most skillful mariners in the ancient world.

❧

The Punic Wars started in Sicily. Carthaginian merchant vessels had been using Sicily as a stopping point on their way to nations along the Northern Mediterranean. Earlier, Carthage had a settlement in Sicily for use in their mercantile endeavors.

Because it wanted to become the major maritime power in the Mediterranean, Rome craved possession of Sicily. In the year 264 BC, Romans annexed one of its major ports, Messina. When the king of Messina called upon Carthage to help, a Carthaginian fleet sailed north under the leadership of Hamilcar Barca, the father of the notorious Hannibal. Unfortunately, Carthage itself was strained by sporadic battles with its neighbors in North Africa, so Hamilcar's ships were severely undermanned. Because of that, Hamilcar wasn't successful. The king of Sicily lost control of Messina, and later all of Sicily as well as Corsica, Sardinia and the Aegate Islands.

BATTLE OF CAPE ECONOMUS

When Hamilcar retreated from Sicily, his naval fleet moved Westward in the Mediterranean, but met up with a mighty Roman fleet who were in hot pursuit. The Carthaginian ships then moved into their traditional horseshoe-shaped formation. However, the Romans configured their vessels into a wedge shape. Then they tore at the Carthaginian ships, realigned themselves into a semicircle, and eventually had the Carthaginian ships virtually surrounded. Because they lost so many vessels in this conflagration, Carthage had to surrender and Hamilcar left for Carthage.

There were several other pertinent battles at sea and on land between Rome and Carthage. Consul Atilius Regulus in Rome decided to take the war to Carthage in Africa under his own command. Regulus staged a couple of surprise attacks on Carthaginian properties in Clupea and Tunis and won. Hamilcar was then called back to assist. He did so, but his troops were depleted due to problems with the mercenary soldiers he had hired for the battles on land. They were still in Sicily awaiting orders from the Carthaginian authorities. In addition, they hadn't been paid and were furious about the delay with their departure. Carthage was beginning to have financial difficulties.

⚜

Next, Carthage recruited another mercenary, Xanthippus. Xanthippus was an excellent commander and rescued Carthage from the Roman sieges. He also marched upon Tunis and recaptured the city handily. Even Regulus himself was taken captive! Carthage prevailed in the North African campaign, but was still in a dire financial condition. The First Punic War ended in the year 247 BC.

SECOND PUNIC WAR

※※※

According to the treaty Carthage and Rome made, Rome agreed not to conquer lands in Spain that lay SouthWest of the Ebro River. However, wishing to discourage Carthage from conquering Spain, the clever Romans allied themselves with the territories around the city of Sanguntum (now called **"Sagunto"** in Valencia province). Rome had also built immense fortifications there for the protection of the Saguntines.

※※※

HANNIBAL AND THE BATTLE OF SANGUNTUM

※※※

The notorious general, Hannibal, was the son of Hamilcar

and put in charge of the troops. When he was a boy, Hannibal's father had him make this pledge:

> *"I swear, as soon as age will permit, I will use fire and metal to arrest the destiny of Rome."*

In 219 BC, Hannibal and the Carthaginian troops stormed into Sanguntum. The Carthaginians needed food, money and supplies. Discovering Roman fortifications there, Hannibal and his men dismantled them. Then they plundered the city. When the ravaged population capitulated, Hannibal told everyone to leave unarmed and take only two garments with them. After the Sanguntines rejected that outrageous proposal, Hannibal slaughtered all the men and led the women and children into slavery.

ॐ

CROSSING OF THE ALPS AND THE BATTLE OF TREBIA

ॐ

To elude the Romans, Hannibal attempted to give Rome the impression that he was going to concentrate his efforts in Gaul. He didn't. Instead, he hired Gallic mercenaries and moved toward Italy. Brashly, he and his troops mounted the rocky crags of the Alps. Hannibal had with him forty elephants as well. During the crossing, he lost nearly half his men to the treacherous narrow passes of the peaks. All but a few elephants died. It was winter of the year 218 BC. After perilously descending the Alps, Hannibal caught the Roman legions by surprise. Consul Sempronius Longus headed up the

Roman forces. His force was well-manned and well-supplied but Sempronius was inexperienced and immature. When he and his men were confronted by the elephants, they panicked and retreated without orders to do so. Rome was appalled. Rome then recalled Sempronius and put Consul Flaminius II in charge. That was likewise unsuccessful. Flaminius was killed at a battle near Lake Trasimeme and quickly replaced.

༄༅

BATTLE OF CANNAE

༄༅

After the winter had passed, and the Carthaginians troops had been depleted by a number of smaller skirmishes conducted by Consul Varro, who was then at the head of the forces. In Spring, Varro chose the open plains of Cannae to encounter Hannibal himself.

༄༅

During the first phase of the battle, the Roman infantrymen had to deal with the wind and the dust that blew up from the dry fields. When they saw Hannibal tighten up his ranks, the Romans charged at him full-force. Breaking off one flank to the right and the other to the left, the Romans surrounded his troops.

༄༅

Hannibal's brother, Hasdrubal was also raging through Italy up the coast. He had taken some of the smaller towns and villages there, and was marching Northward to join up with Hannibal. He had many heavy cavalry forces manned by the talented mercenary Numidian horsemen. Hasdrubal then attacked the Romans from behind. The Roman troops were jammed between Hannibal and Hasdrubal and were mercilessly slaughtered. By the battle's end, bodies lay on top of one another on the blood-soaked ground. This was a resounding victory for the Carthaginian troops, despite the fact that their numbers were less than ideal.

SENATOR CATO THE ELDER:
"CARTHAGE MUST BE
DESTROYED!"

❧

Hannibal wanted to conquer Rome but lacked siege engines to mount city walls. He knew he would need those, as well as much more heavy-duty military equipment for the attack. Repeatedly, Hannibal sent messages back to Carthage for reinforcements and supplies. None came. Why? Because Rome had also dispatched a fleet and armed troops under the capable leadership of Consul Publius Scipio – also known as **Scipio Africanus**.

❧

Carthage had long ago been plagued by rebellions to the East and South of the city of Carthage itself. Its territories and colonies were much smaller than those of mighty Rome. While Hannibal and Hasdrubal had been engaged in Southern Europe and the Italian peninsula, Carthage couldn't control its home city. Hannibal was then called home to defend Carthage and its possessions. At the city of Zama (in today's Tunisia) he and Scipio met in a ferocious battle. Rome's soldiers were highly skilled with infantry operations, while Hannibal's forces consisted mostly of mercenaries and citizen soldiers. Rome easily won the Battle of Zama. Hannibal, who had once called himself the **"Scourge of God,"** deserted. The year was 202 BC and that marked the end of the Second Punic War.

THE THIRD PUNIC WAR – THE
BATTLE OF CARTHAGE 149 BC

᭓᭓᭓

A call came from the floor of Roman Senate to assure that Rome would never more have to deal with the Carthaginian threat. Scipio Africanus Aemilianus, grandson of the great Scipio Africanus, responded.

᭓᭓᭓

Carthage was in severe financial straits at that time, but fought back hardily and had some victories. However, when Scipio Aemilianus arrived, he placed Carthage under siege. The Fall and Winter of that year was brutal, and the city defenders were starving. They had very few workable weapons left. In the year 146 BC, Scipio permit the residents and unarmed defenders to leave. Then the Romans set fire to the city. After two days, the city was nothing more than cinders and stones. The Third Punic War was over in the year 146 BC.

"HAIL, CAESAR!"

༺❊༻

By the First Century AD, Rome had essentially subjected many lands to their exclusive control:

- Italy
- Spain (Iberia)
- France (Gaul)
- Southern England (Anglia)
- Greece and the Greek peninsula
- Turkey (Bithynia)
- Egypt
- North Africa

༺❊༻

Each province had their own Rome-appointed governor and legions of well-equipped Roman legions to control and guide the populations. All of them paid taxes fees and levies to Rome.

✿

In Rome itself, there were periods of great discord during the reigns of Marius (104 BC – 100 BC) and Sulla (88 BC – 80 BC) who was both consuls and later dictators. Both were bloodthirsty tyrants who competed with each other. Sulla even attacked the city itself in an effort to seize power. During the course of his reign, Sulla made grandiose changes to the governmental and the military structure of Rome. He also confiscated the property of many, including the plebeians.

✿

The Plebeian Assembly, was at that time more powerful than the assemblage representing the patrician nobles. Many of the Plebeian leaders were assassinated by agents of Marius and Sulla. Unrest and chaos ruled the streets. There was also a slave rebellion led by the gladiator, Spartacus. Rome was a war with itself!

✿

Around 71 AD, the Roman Republic started to wane, but the end had not yet come.

✿

From this turbulence, arose Gaius Julius Caesar. He had a brilliant career in the military, and his victories abroad made him famous. His physical appearance was handsome and

39

strong, and he was the personification of a strong hero. The people loved him.

❧❧❧

THE FIRST TRIUMVIRATE – ITS RISE AND FALL

❧❧❧

Realizing that another form of government was sorely needed, Caesar joined up with influential power brokers at the time – Marcus Lucinius Crassus, Gnaeus Pompeius Magnus (Pompey) and himself. The year was 59 BC.

❧❧❧

Rome was still expanding and Crassus was in the East fighting for the domination of Rome. The Parthians (tribe located in today's Turkey) killed him during battle. Pompey argued vehemently with Caesar because he wanted more power. He and Caesar engaged in battle, and Pompey fled, only to be murdered in Egypt. Caesar then left Rome for military campaigns in Spain and Egypt. Upon his return, the Senate awarded him many honors for expanding Roman territories.

JULIUS CAESAR – DICTATOR
FOR LIFE

ॐ

Caesar strengthened the government but reduced the power of the Senate. He regulated grain prices and appointed new senators. He then granted himself veto power over new legislation and approval of the election of public officials. Roman citizens appreciated his administrative abilities. Caesar brought prosperity back to Rome and was given the grandiose title **"Imperator"** as result. He even provided entertainment for the masses at the great Circus Maximus. When he traveled, the people celebrated his leadership with grand parades, shouting

"Hail, Caesar!"

The year was 44 BC.

ASSASSINATION!

❦

Caesar luxuriated within this ground swelling of worshipping people, but the Senators became jealous and angry. Caesar was considered a **"god"**. Because Caesar had diminished the power of the Senate, Senators felt that they had lost the respect of the people. Jealousy festered within their minds and hearts. It increased to the point that they conspired among themselves to rid Rome of Caesar.

❦

In order to put their plot in motion, the Senators called Caesar to a meeting within the Senate. His first task upon arrival was to hear petitions from the people. As he sat upon his stone chair, a man by the name of Timber Cimba stepped forward, accompanied by Marcus Casca. Without warning, they grabbed Caesar and wrestled him to the ground. Inundated with avarice and rage, nearly sixty Senators closed in on his prone form. Brutally, they stabbed him repeatedly. Horrified by their own barbaric act, they rushed out of the Senate building. Caesar's bloodied body lay there in a lifeless heap for three hours.

The date was the **"Ides of March,"** that is, March 15, 44 BC.

❧ III ❧
ANCIENT ROME –
EMPERORS, ABLE
OR INEPT

44 BC – 222 AD FROM AUGUSTUS TO ELAGABALUS

⚜

I'm never less at leisure than when at leisure, or less alone than when alone.

Scipio Africanus

⚜

AN OMINOUS WARNING OF THE COMING TURMOIL

❦

ccording to Virgil in his poem *Georgics,* there was an eclipse on the day after Caesar's assassination,

> *"Who dare say the Sun is false? He and no other*
> *warns us when a dark uprising threatens, when*
> *treachery and hidden wars are gathering*
> *strength. He and no other was moved to pity*
> *Rome on the day that Caesar died. When he*
> *unveiled his radiance in gloom and darkness, a*
> *godless age feared everlasting night."*

❦

THE SECOND TRIUMVIRATE

※

During the interim following Caesar's assassination, Mark Antony, one of Caesar's military commanders had temporary stewardship of Rome. As part of the Second Triumvirate, Julius Caesar's adopted son and heir, Octavian was appointed. He was a military leader from the Plebeian classes and a skillful horseman. He and Antony then recruited Marcus Aemilius Lepidus and established the Second Triumvirate. There was a great deal of unrest and disorder among the people of Rome. If anarchy ensued from that, it would have repercussions in all the Roman territories.

※

New senators needed to be appointed to replace the assassins who fled Rome. Guards needed to be set in place to restore order and provide some stability so that the business of government and commerce could once again flourish.

※

DEFEAT AND CAPTURE OF THE "LIBERATORES"

※

To prevent any further deterioration of the well-organized government of Rome, Antony and Octavian put Lepidus in charge of the Italy and spearheaded an effort to capture and punish the assassins of Caesar, who then called themselves the **"Liberatores."** Brutus and Cassius Longinus, the two main conspirators, and their troops engaged the triumvirs, Octavian and Antony twice at Phillippi, located in Macedonia. After two years of battle, both Cassius and Brutus were captured. Cassius and Brutus committed suicide rather than undergo execution. The year was 42 BC.

❧

After that event, the three triumvirs frequently quarreled about the scope of their responsibilities. In an attempt to secure more power and popular support, Lepidus managed to stir up a rebellion in Sicily. As result, Octavian reduced him to a lower rank and eventually sent him into exile. Mark Antony was appointed the leader of the Eastern territories of the Roman world. While there, he initiated a number of military campaigns to conquer new colonies and make them subservient to Rome. Despite Antony's military accomplishments, the people and Senators in Rome still preferred Octavian to Antony. In an effort to ingratiate himself to Octavian and the Romans, Antony married Octavian's daughter, Octavia. However, during his campaign in Egypt, he became romantically involved with Queen Cleopatra and consequently deserted his grief-stricken wife. Antony rejected the charge of desertion when Octavian confronted him. Because the power brokers in Rome feared a repeat of Caesar's reign as a **"god,"** they supported Mark Antony. Even the powerful Senator, Cicero, was in allegiance with him. Backed by such an influential following and military forces as well, Antony declared war against Octavian in 31 BC.

THE BATTLE OF ACTIUM

❦

Octavian met up with Antony's fleet in the Gulf of Actium off Greece. Cleopatra also contributed some of her swifter Egyptian vessels along with weapons and provisions for the men. Antony used the standard Roman ships, quinqueremes. They were heavily loaded with weapons and fighting men. Octavian's naval fleet was composed of *Liburnas*, which were smaller but highly maneuverable. As the opposing ships slammed into each other broadside, a seaman by the name of Quintus Delius betrayed Antony. He leaped on to Octavian's flagship taking Antony's battle plans with him. Octavian, using Antony's battle plans, altered his strategy and pulled some of his ships away from the close encounter Antony had strategized. When Antony's troops saw the tide turning in favor of Octavian, many Antony's men defected. Once Cleopatra saw that Antony was losing, she pulled her vessels away from the action. Antony's fleet followed her, and Mark Antony himself was hoisted aboard Cleopatra's flagship. Crushed by defeat, Mark Antony fled to Egypt with her.

❧

As sole ruler in Rome, Octavian took the name of Augustus Caesar, meaning **"the illustrious one."**

❧

This marked the end of the Roman Republic and the beginning of "The Roman Empire." The year was 27 BC.

THE ROMAN EMPIRE IS BORN

❧

A ny understanding of the causes for the rise and fall of a nation or empire rests upon its leadership throughout time. With the collapse of a civilization comes the destruction of its values and culture. If a civilization is successful, its principles are forever enshrined within the people of future generations.

THE ILLUSTRIOUS ONE,
AUGUSTUS CAESAR – REIGN 17
BC-14 AD

༺❀༻

J ulius Caesar made the error of assuming overwhelming power. Augustus did not. He never wanted to be declared **"Emperor."** Instead he preferred to be known as a *Princeps*, that is, **"Prince."** He stated that his powers were like those of a tribune (see below), but with some additional privileges such as the right to participate in consular discussions, the right to speak in the Senate, the right to propose laws, the right to veto a law and the right to grant amnesty to an individual. Early on, he decided he would only selectively use those powers.

༺❀༻

The structure of the Roman government was derived through the interaction of the various roles of its officials. Although the **"Constitution of Rome"** was actually an unwritten document, history indicates that it consisted of the following:

- **Emperor** – The Emperor was responsible for the smooth operation of the government in Rome and foreign affairs.
- **Consuls** – Two consuls were elected per year to serve jointly. They basically laid out the business for consideration of matters related the other sectors – military, legislative, foreign relations, taxes and domestic policies concerning moral behavior (as opposed to religion, *per se*)
- **Tribunes** – maintain a balance of power between the patrician and plebeians in Rome, convene the Senate if needed, and deal with matters of justice and appeal of sentences
- **Provincial Governors** – These governors were the administrators of the provinces of Rome outside the city itself. Duties included justice, tax collection and security.
- **Senate** – The Senate provided the impetus for stability and progress. The senators argued the issues of the day and passed legislation recommended by the people's assemblies (Patricians and Plebeians). They regulated the tax system and treasury.

PAX ROMANA (ROMAN PEACE)

❦

U nlike the leaders during the Roman Republic, Augustus turned his attention to Rome itself. He noted that the public squares had become dirty and neglected. They were peopled with squatters, and most Roman citizens veered away from them for fear of crime. Many of the structures were worn and dilapidated. The main Forum had fallen into disarray. Augustus restored it and built a great arch. He wanted foreign traders to come to Rome, so he encouraged the public to sell their produce and wares. Although Rome still used the more ancient silver coins, Augustus introduced brass and copper. To this day, tourists can still see green stains on the cobblestones of the Roman Forum from these coins.

❦

Augustus wanted his people to be moral and maintain high principles. During his reign, he erected new temples dedicated to Appollo, Vesta, Jupiter and Mars. The enormous Pantheon stands sentinel in Rome and is home to all the gods of Rome. Although it was later altered by Emperor Hadrian in 132 AD, its columns and foundation date back to 27 BC when Augustus was emperor. History records the very words of Augustus regarding the architectural beauty he brought to Rome:

"I found Rome built of brick but left it marble."

❧

This was a time of great peace when ancient scholars, historians and poets used their skills to educate and enlighten the people. Livy's histories, Horace's odes, Ovid's elegies and Strabo's geographies were written during the time of Augustus, and so was Virgil's *Aeneid*. (see Chapter 1)

❧

Recalling the grievous offense committed by Mark Antony by abandoning his daughter, Augustus reformed the marriage and divorce laws. Adultery became a criminal offense.

❧

Tax and inheritance laws were rewritten and became more fair. Augustus had officials appointed who would manage the income and expenditures of Rome. This reduced bribery and usury on the part of merchants and nobles as well as the general population.

❧

Caesar Augustus fostered religious tolerance throughout the Empire. During his reign, Christianity was born in the Eastern provinces around 1-6 AD with the birth of its founder, Jesus Christ.

⚙

Upon his deathbed, Augustus said to his wife, Livia,

> *"Have I played the part well? If so, then applaud as I exit."*

The year was 14 AD.

THE TWO FACES OF CALIGULA –
REIGN 37-41 AD

ॐ

The given name of this emperor was Gaius Julius Caesar Germanicus. **"Caligula"** was a nickname given to him because of the small sandals, called *caligae,* that he wore when playing war games as a child.

ॐ

In the interest of full disclosure and transparency, he published the governmental budget. He repaired aqueducts, abolished excessive taxes for the common people, improved the military and raised their salaries, established an **"insurance"** system to help compensate people for losses incurred due to fires (which were common in the 1st Century) and contributed a great deal to public entertainment events. Gladiators fought in the arenas to thrill the crowds and chariot races were regularly held. There were gigantic spectacles of battles and sports events. In addition, he created a system of free elections for government offices. Caligula was extremely popular among the people.

***

Then, in the year 39 AD, he changed dramatically. Caligula charged a number of Senators with immoral conduct and collusion. He punished them, and even executed some. In mockery, Caligula had his own horse appointed as consul.

***

In order to enhance his pleasures, he sometimes forced spectators at the games into the arena to be attacked and consumed by wild beasts. He was hedonistic and even had prostitutes at his royal court. He himself was incestuous and a known adulterer.

***

Because of Caligula's enormous expenditures, Rome acquired a massive debt. Taxes were then raised and the lack of money in circulation caused starvation. Famine is often followed by disease. Large segments of the population died.

***

In the year 40 AD, he was assassinated by his own Praetorian guard.

THE HONEST CONQUEROR,
VESPASIAN – REIGN 69-79 AD

❦

Vespasian was a military man. Prior to his entry on the world stage, he assisted Rome in conquering a larger segment of Britain, expanding the Empire Northward up to Scotland. His goal was to expand and solidify the Roman Empire. Former Roman emperors often extorted money from the wealthy in the territories they invaded, but Vespasian was different. While on his North African campaign, he befriended many although his odd sense of humor sometimes lost him the respect of the tribes who mocked him. On one occasion, the ancient historians relate that the people threw turnips at him!

❦

While still young, Vespasian always paid his debts. Because he fostered good relationships in North Africa, those who could, gave him loans. In order to pay those off, he even drove a team of mules for various landowners!

Vespasian subdued the territories of Dalmatia and Moesia (north of Greece). The Romans back home had been enduring food shortages due to the civil wars that erupted during Nero's reign that preceded his. First of all, Vespasian resolved that by securing grain shipments from Egypt which he conquered in 70 AD. In addition, he also increased the amount of the tributes conquered nations paid to Rome.

Much of his reign was spent in crushing rebellions. He delegated his son, Titus, to subdue the Jewish rebellion in Palestine. In the year 70 AD, the temple of Solomon was destroyed. That horrendous event will forever be recorded by both the Jews and the Christians.

At the age of 69, he was extremely ill and on his deathbed. However, he insisted that he die standing up as an Emperor should. His assistants helped him to his feet and then he collapsed and died. The year was 79 AD.

THE HELLENISTIC HISPANIC,
HADRIAN – REIGN 117-138 AD

๖๏๙

Hadrian was born in Italica, Hispania (Seville, Spain today). Hadrian spent most of his life traveling about the Roman Empire inspecting his legions who protected the various provinces of Rome. History records that he mingled with the soldiers and slept with them at their encampments.

๖๏๙

Hadrian is noted for the construction of **"Hadrian's Wall"** in England. It is a great stone wall punctuated with fortifications intended to prevent barbaric tribes from pillaging the farms of the Anglian country people. Sections of this wall still exist today.

๖๏๙

૭ૐૹ

Upon his early visits to Greece, Hadrian developed a love of the Greek (Hellenistic) culture and literature. He became an initiate in the *Eleusinian Mysteries,* a secretive religious cult that worshipped Demeter, the goddess of fertility and agriculture. The poet, Homer, wrote a hymn to her saying,

> *"She is more lovely than a daffodil by a stone wall. I*
> *gaze on her for hours and hours until I fall into a*
> *trance and worship her; Earth, mother of all."*

Initiates like Hadrian were participants in the sacred rituals at which they performed animal sacrifices. History scholars have been investigating the Eleusinian Mysteries for years.

૭ૐૹ

Even though Hadrian ranks among those who were called the **"Five Good Emperors,"** he didn't maintain peaceful relations with the Jewish people. In the year 130 AD, he descended upon Palestine. It was which was in ruins since prior wars with the Romans. Hadrian then built his own temple on the site of Solomon's temple and triggered off Kokhbah's Revolt. That was a vicious guerilla-style conflagration after which Hadrian was victorious. Hadrian's men then followed it up by the sadistic torture of the Jews. Historians indicate that Hadrian also forbade Judaism and banned the *Torah.* Reportedly, he also destroyed some Christian sites as well. He renamed the territory Syria Palestinia after their ancient enemies, the Philistines.

❧

Hadrian, like so many rulers of the ancient and medieval world, experienced many conflicts over his succession because he was childless. He brutally executed many who were contenders of his throne. Before one of them – Servianus – was executed, Servianus said he hoped Hadrian would "long for death but be unable to die." Victimized by a prolonged illness, that curse came true. Hadrian passed away in 138 AD.

THE SUPERSTITIOUS EMPEROR, SEPTIMIUS SEVERUS – REIGN 193-211 AD

❧

Septimius was a ruthless warrior and conqueror who ended his reign with a prolonged period of peace. He always believed he would be emperor because of visions and omens. As a young man, he had a dream that he was being nursed by a wolf, like Remus and Romulus. Severus sought glory and control. His first military campaign as emperor occurred in Parthia located in today's Iraq and Iran. He treated his men mercilessly and disease raged through his troops. The Roman legions, despite that, were victorious and the Parthian king was sent into exile.

❧

Septimius executed those he felt might be serious rivals or conspirators, even among his own ranks. In the year 205 AD, he executed Plautianus, his own praetor prefect and son-in-law because of a suspected plot to undermine the emperor's family.

In Rome, his dictatorial demeanor and harsh diatribes alienated the Senate. He even condemned some to death for speaking out against him. By law, the Senators were permitted the right of free expression, but Severus chose to ignore that. Even so, they tolerated him for the most part because of his abilities in handling rebellions and shoring up the defenses of the Empire, especially in Britain.

Those whom he considered his political rivals were sometimes executed without a trial. When Septimius wrote his autobiography, he attempted to rationalize his bad reputation for cruelty.

The people of Rome felt differently. They loved him, as he stamped out the corruption that infiltrated the moneylenders and merchants. Septimius also gave everyone an allotment of oil free of charge, much to their delight. In the city, he built the Baths of Severus, remnants of which still remain today. During his reign, he promoted efficient and intelligent leaders within Rome on the basis of merit. When he dwelled in Rome toward the latter half of his life, peace prevailed. Many people chose to forget the tales of his cruelty in the past.

Severus became deathly ill during his last military engagement in Caledonia (current-day Scotland). He is said to have had portents and omens predicting his death. On one occasion, he said he had a vision of himself being carried up to the heavens by the great god Jupiter. Suetonius, the ancient historian, said of him,

"Never was there a better servant or worse master."

The year was 211 AD.

THE DEPRAVED BOY EMPEROR,
ELAGABALUS – REIGN 218-222 AD

౫ళ౬

H is name was actually Marcus Aurelius Antoninus Augustus upon his accession to Emperor. Elagabalus is a nickname and the one by which he is known throughout history. He was given that name because of his mind-crazed devotion to the Syrian sun god, Elagabul.

౫ళ౬

For his overture, he committed the public offense of replacing Jupiter, the godhead of the Pantheon, with Elagabul. During his rule, he partook in sex orgies in the temples and even married a Vestal Virgin, which was forbidden by the religious code of Rome. Then he forced members of the gentry and Senate to proclaim their belief in his obscure Syrian god. Ceremonies in the temple were accompanied by the clash of cymbals and the thunder of drums.

❧❧

Reportedly, he conducted child sacrifices in the solemn buildings of Rome and engaged in sex in the temples. The boy had no interest in matters of state and permit his grandmother, Maesa, to govern Rome.

❧❧

In 222 AD, he was assassinated by his own Praetor guards.

❦ IV ❦

ANCIENT ROME –
DIVISION, DECLINE &
DEATH

222 AD – 476 AD FROM EXPANSION TO EXPLOSION

❦

*Advice in old age is foolish; for what can be more absurd than
to increase our provisions for the road the nearer we approach
to our journey's end.*

Marcus Tullius Cicero

❦

THIRD CENTURY CRISIS

❦

D uring the 3rd Century, discord erupted in Rome and spread throughout the Empire from a multitude of sources:

- ***Increase in Military Control*** – Very often, military commanders craved control of the Empire. Between the years of 235-284 AD, twenty-six people claimed the title of Emperor! Anarchy and individualism took the place of the traditional command structure. Military officers sometimes assassinated Emperors, such as was the case with Egalabalus in the prior chapter. His successor, Alexander Severus, was also slaughtered by his own troops in 235 AD.
- ***Economic Depression*** – When plagues occurred during the centuries, people abandoned their farms for want of laborers. Others were forced to leave

due to erosion or climactic factors. Devaluation of the currency occurred as the nations had to turn back to more primitive metals for coinage.

- *Barbaric Invasions* – This was the migratory period during which tribes increased in population and its members sought new sources to provide for themselves and their families. So they infringed on the borders, plundered the farms and villages, and killed many.

- *The Size and Scope of the Roman Empire* – At its height of its expansion, the Roman Empire encompassed 6,500,000 km² or over 2 million square miles. The populations of the provinces had been continually growing at an exponential rate. Administration of such an unwieldly area was impossible.

- *The High Turnover of Emperors* – Between the years of 238 and 253 AD most of the Emperors served for a period of one month to two years! Most of them died at the hands of military assassins or in battles between military factions.

THE REIGN OF VALERIAN AND
GALLIENUS – 253-268 AD

❧

The Roman Senate recognized the importance of dividing imperial responsibilities for such a vast Empire. Valerian ruled in the East and Gallienus ruled the West.

❧

VALERIAN IN THE EAST

❧

The Eastern powers of the Sassinids, a massive Persian tribe, had gained control of the territories encompassing the MidEast, Syria, the Levant and segments of Egypt. These were fierce Arab tribes.

❧

BATTLE OF EDESSA – VALERIAN CAPTURED!

❧

The Sassanids were led by King Shapur I in 260 AD. They met the Roman legions at Edessa, now located in Eastern Turkey. The Sassinids were experienced desert warriors who used *Sythai* – curved swords – and slashed at their enemies from horseback. Valerian was beaten and dragged into captivity. There are many conflicting histories as to his manner of death ranging from being forced to swallow molten gold to being flayed alive.

GALLIENUS IN THE WEST

✦

In the Western portion of the Empire, the greatest threat to unity came from the intrusions of the Germanic tribes from areas lying West of the Rhine River, the Franks in the area of the lower Rhine, current-day France and Spain. From East of the Rhine, the Alammani, a Germanic tribe had mustered control of Dalmatia, Moesia (Northern Greek peninsula) and later they threatened Italy itself.

✦

MILITARY REFORM UNDER GALLIENUS

✦

Gallienus established specialized swift cavalry units in the military to quell the barbarians from the Northern and

Eastern borders in particular. Up until then, Rome had just been stationing troops along its borders rather than placing them in critical inland areas.

⚜

In addition, Gallienus also forbade Senators from becoming military commanders. That curtailed the overwhelming power the Senators had gained through the years.

⚜

Unfortunately, this wasn't enough to prevent Roman usurpers from conquering portions of the Roman Empire.

⚜

GALLIENUS AND THE REVOLT OF INGENUUS

⚜

Ingenuus was a former Military Commander in charge of Pannonia (in the Northern Greek peninsula). He rebelled against the central authority of Rome when Gallenius was in Gaul dealing with the Germanic tribes. After dismantling institutions of the Roman authorities, Ingenuus declared himself Emperor. Gallienus quickly returned and confronted him at the city of Mursa (in today's Croatia) and handily defeated him there.

⚜

GALLIENUS AT THE BATTLE OF MEDIOLANUM 259 AD

❀

Directly following the encounter with Ingenuus, the Senate called upon Gallienus' military prowess. The Alamanni, a Germanic tribe, was moving South and invaded Milan. Although the Alamanni had far more soldiers under their command, they were less organized than the Roman legions. With the use of three legions, Gallienus defeated them there. This battle helped Rome reunite the areas North of Italy with the Germanic provinces in the area.

❀

CONSPIRACIES OF ROMAN COMMANDERS – MURDER OF GALLIENUS!

❀

As testimony the the earlier discussion regarding the rising power of the Roman military commanders, Emperor Gallienus had to deal with usurpers among his own troops. In Eastern Turkey, the Roman commander, Macrianus revolted. In Gaul, Aureolus and Posthumus, both Roman officers, rebelled. Gallienus defeated them, but that was only temporary. Posthumus gathered new supportive forces and murdered Gallienus. The year was 268 AD.

THE TETRARCHY

҉

Establishment of a **"Tetrarchy"** in 293 AD during the reign of Diocletian effectively ended the crisis in the 3rd Century.

҉

A Tetrarchy means the rule of a territory under four leaders. Because the Empire was so massive, and there was a myriad of different factors that affected the growth and welfare of the people, it was necessary to reorganize the Roman administration.

҉

The new Emperor, Diocletian, separated the Roman Empire into four divisions Empire with capitals that were removed from Rome proper.

❦

The Four Areas:

- ***Viennensis*** + ***Britanniae*** + ***Gallia*** – included what is known today as France, Western Germany and Britain. Its capital was Augusta Treverorum (in Germany).
- ***Hispania*** + ***Africa*** + ***Italia*** – included today's Spain, the NorthWestern African coast and Italy. Its capital was Mediolanum (Milan).
- ***Pannoniae*** + ***Moesia*** + ***Thrace*** – included the Balkan States and the Greek peninsula. Its capital was Sirmium (Belgrade).
- ***Oriens*** + ***Asiana*** + ***Pontica*** – included NorthEastern Africa, and a portion of Egypt, the Eastern Mediterranean coastal countries of Palestine, Judea, Syria and Turkey. Its capital was Nicomedia (in Turkey).

❦

While the division of power under the Tetrarchy seemed to be a workable system, it disintegrated during succession disputes and a string of usurpers within the Empire. By the year 313, the Roman Empire was split into two separate areas – the East, headed up by Lucinius and the West headed by Constantine the Great.

EMPEROR DIOCLETIAN AND THE
ONSET OF THE CHRISTIAN
PERSECUTIONS

⚜

A t the very onset of the Tetrarchy, an edict forbidding the practice of the Christian religion was passed by Diocletion and approved by the other three Emperors, Maximian, Gallerius and Constantius. This **"Constantius"** is not to be confused with Constantine the Great, one of his descendants. In Nicomedia, capital of Eastern segment of the Tetrarchy, Christian churches were destroyed and their sacred writings burned on the orders of Diocletian. This emperor was pagan and felt that the stability of his region depended upon the unification of belief systems surrounding the traditional Roman gods. Anyone professing to be Christian could not hold public office and lost their rights originally granted under the Plebeian Assembly. Although Diocletian wanted those judicial actions to be undertaken without bloodshed, that wasn't always the case. Another emperor, Gallerius, who ruled areas around the Greek peninsula, countermanded those orders and had many Christians burned alive. Clergymen and bishops were regularly imprisoned.

⚜

However, in time, the prisons became difficult to administer when they became overcrowded. To resolve that, the emperors issued orders that a clergyman could be freed if he sacrificed to a Roman god. Some did, but many didn't. Upon receiving those orders, many of the wardens falsified documents to alleviate the overcrowding. Some, of course, were sympathizers or clandestine Christians themselves.

⚜

More edicts were passed, even ones requiring that all the people gather in their public squares and offer animal sacrifices. Those who refused were immediately executed.

⚜

In the year 313, Gallerius had the Edict of Milan passed and approved. It promoted benevolence toward the Christians. However, all their properties were confiscated.

DECADENCE AND DECAY OF THE
ROMAN EMPIRE

❧

Properties of Christians and criminals had been confiscated during the Tetrarchy. Taxes were raised on the owned properties to the point that vast acres were abandoned. Cities and towns lacked the financial resources to provide effective administration for the people. The central authorities of Rome became politically corrupt when higher magistrates distributed much of the city's wealth to their family, friends and allies.

❧

Payments to the regular military was severely reduced as less and less taxes could be collected. To compensate, they extorted money from the public. As the coinage devalued, soldiers were often paid in land rather than currency. Many were forced to resort to farming, but had little experience in doing so. Military discipline broke down. The intrusions of invaders at the borders of the Empire caused an unwise focus upon defending the borders, neglecting the cities and towns. Troops of bandits wandered through the countryside pillaging and leaving scorched earth behind them. Public services all but ceased.

BARBARIC INVASIONS- THE
VISIGOTHS

๛

The Visigoths were Germanic tribes that found their origin around the Black Sea. Having spent many years in the Northern Germanic territories they spoke a distinctive Germanic language. In the year 250 AD, they invaded Anatolia (Turkey) in the Eastern Roman Empire. From there, they moved into the Greek peninsula pillaging as they went.

๛

Emperor Valens ruled the Eastern Roman Empire from 364 -378 AD. After word of the Visigoths' attack in Anatolia (Turkey), Valens took 20,000 troops with him and marched to Adrianople. It was a challenging terrain filled with rocks and rivers. After marching seven hours, Valens and his men were inundated with smoke from fires the enemy had set to obscure their vision. Having gone through a prolonged period that lack the usual military drills and discipline, the Romans were at a distinct disadvantage. At this battle, some legionnaires rushed forward without orders to do so. When the Romans engaged the Visigoths at Adrianople in hand-to-hand combat, the more adept Gothic cavalrymen raced toward them. That battle raged on all day, and hundreds of Romans were slaughtered. Their formations no longer existed, and Roman corpses were scattered all over the countryside. Emperor Valens never emerged after there was a call for negotiations. His body was never found.

⬥

ALARIC – KING OF THE VISIGOTHS AND EMPEROR HONORIUS

⬥

During the reign of Flavius Honorius, the Visigoth king initiated three sieges of Rome. Desirous of some land in Italy in order to create a Visigoth Kingdom, Alaric tried to negotiate with Honorius. Even though the people in Rome were half-starved and disease was rampant, the stubborn Honorius rejected Alaric's terms. Then the Visigoths renewed their siege and penetrated Rome. They sacked the city and forced the population into slavery. Emperor Honorius now had to draw up a treaty with the Visigoths. As result, the Visigoths were granted in a strip of territory East of the Tiber River and a large portion of land in Southern Gaul and Iberia (Spain).

⬥

The Roman Empire had now lost North Eastern seacoast of Italy, Southern Gaul (France) and Spain, but at least there was peace between the Visigoths and Rome.

BARBARIC INVASIONS –
THE HUNS

꘠꘠꘠

The Huns originally heralded from the Caucasus region (Russia) and ethnic tribes from the Han Empire in China. They were fierce warriors who fought on horseback. These rough and primitive warriors raced Westward, conquering huge swaths of territory. Their practice wasn't to occupy those lands, but to extort huge payments called **"tributes."** Under the leadership of the notorious leader, Attila (434-453 AD), they had subdued areas in the Balkans, Moesia in the Northern Greek peninsula and Western Anatolia (Turkey). Next, they headed toward Gaul.

꘠꘠꘠

Hunnic soldiers were required to bring their own provisions with them. Their combat forces took herds of cattle and goats with them for food. Huns ate raw meat and drank the milk of goats. When they consumed all of their own animals, they plundered farms and stole barnyard animals as well as grain and crops.

☙❧

EMPEROR VALENTINIAN'S SCANDAL

☙❧

The Emperor had a daughter, Honoria, who had a reputation for sexual promiscuity. The Roman Senate complained bitterly as this was totally unacceptable according to the code of morality they practiced, and an embarrassment to the Roman Empire. To remedy the situation, Valentinian begged an elderly Senator to marry her. He agreed but demanded the remaining lands in the Western Roman Empire as his dowry! Of course, that wasn't acceptable, so Valentinian debated with himself as to whether to send Honoria to a convent or secretly have her murdered.

☙❧

In the meantime, Honoria was horrified at the prospect of being married to an old man. In a fit of anxiety-ridden frustration, the immature girl sent her ring to Attila, asking him to intercede.

☙❧

Attila took the gift of the ring to mean that Honoria was proposing marriage to him! Attila then presented his offer to Valentinan, and demanded surrender of the Empire as *his* dowry!

When Valentinian refused, Attila decided to wage war on Rome to claim his bride and take control of the remaining Roman Empire. In preparation, he enlisted allies from among the barbarian tribes:

- **Heruli** (from areas along the Danube River)
- **Rugians** (from around the Baltic Sea and Scandinavia)
- **Franks** (Germanic and mixed racial groups)
- **Burgundians** (from Scandinavia and Eastern Germany)
- **Ostrogoths** (from East of the Rhine River)
- **Alans** (from Central Asia)
- **Thuringians** (from Central Germany)

EMPEROR VALENTINIAN III AND KING THEODORIC I OF THE VISIGOTHS

Desperate for allies to go up against the Huns, the emperor approached King Theodoric with whom he had a treaty since their sack of Rome. King Theodoric agreed and, in the year 451 AD, the Roman Empire and the Visigoths confronted Attila.

Even though Attila's men were inflicted with a plague that had been raging during the last couple of decades, Attila directed his forces toward a large and long field in Northern Gaul and met up with the Roman and Visigoth troops near the city of Chalons.

BATTLE OF THE CHALONS 451 AD

❧

General Flavius Aetius, King Theodoric and his son, Thorismund, led up the attack on behalf of the Roman Empire. The Roman and Visigoth forces (about 80,000 men) fought from late evening and throughout the night. The battle was bloody as the exhausted fighters from both sides hacked and slashed one another. In the dark, soldiers from both sides stumbled over the bodies of fallen men and horses.

❧

When the gruesome battle subsided, Thorismund and a few of his scouts accidentally wandered into the overnight camp of Attila himself. Instantly, the Huns reacted and Thorismund was badly wounded.

❧

In the morning, General Aetius inspected the battleground. There were more that 100,000 dead or dying. There, underneath in a pileup of Visigoth warriors, lay the mutilated corpse of King Theodoric. Upon seeing that, his loyal and saddened soldiers carried his body back reverently.

Because so many of his men were half-starved and besieged with disease, Attila relocated temporarily into the regions to the East. Commander Aetius pursued him for a time, but his soldiers were also sick and exhausted. Eventually, they made their way back to Rome. The outcome of this battle has been labeled inconclusive by historians because it never ended in a treaty or settlement.

ATTILA RETURNS!

☙

For a time, Attila dreamed of returning to Italy to conquer its fertile regions. He also wanted to claim Honoria as his wife, as she was the means by which he could guarantee any treaties he might sign.

☙

In Italy, the seat of government had been moved to Ravenna in Northern Italy for safety reasons and the mustering of defensive forces. In 453 AD, Attila drew up his forces and rampaged Southward into the Po Valley of Northern Italy.

☙

Then his rugged forces tore through Verona, Concordia, Manua, Padua and Milan. Farms and buildings were pillaged and burned after all their foodstuffs had been taken.

Emperor Valentinian III called out again for allies. So many people had been affected by the barbarian invasions, that there were few who could help. Emperor Marcian, the emperor in the Eastern Roman Empire responded by engaging the Huns in their own homeland near the present-day country of Bulgaria. That would distract them and prevent Attila from getting reinforcements.

❧

POPE LEO I MEETS ATTILA THE HUN

❧

Pope Leo, leader of the Catholic faith intervened. Equipped with a simple sword and wearing his clerical robes, he and a small entourage met Attila on an open field. Attila, the ferocious Hun, was extremely impressed by this remarkable show of courage, and withdrew. All the people in the Roman Empire considered the Pope a miracle-worker, and the act has been portrayed in a number of Medieval paintings.

BARBARIAN INVASIONS – THE VANDALS

☙❧

T he Vandals were originally from NorthWestern Britannia (England). They migrated South into the European continent in the year 400 AD. Then they moved Westward and intermarried with the Germanic people. When the Vandals proceeded Westward, they conquered massive territories in Gaul, Iberia, and North Africa.

☙❧

The Mediterranean Sea had been the center of commerce for three continents. However, during this time, Vandals engaged in piracy. That factor alone depleted the shipments of grain, supplies and products such as olive oil and foodstuffs made from dried produce. Because so few products reached the Southern European ports, famines were frequent.

DEATH OF EMPEROR
VALENTINIAN

❧

During the reign of Valentinian III, the Roman Empire had lost control of the Northern Greek peninsula, Germania, Iberia and Gaul (except for a small area in the NorthWest.) After naval raids from the Vandals, the Roman Empire also lost their holdings along the NorthWestern coast of Africa.

❧

The 18th Century historian Edward Gibbon described Valentinian as having **"passions without virtue."** He further stated that Valentinian was a self-indulgent and selfish man. He was grossly incompetent and responsible for the loss of thousands of Roman colonies. In the year 455 AD, he was assassinated.

FINAL DAYS OF THE ROMAN EMPIRE

֍

B y the year 475 AD, one of the Gothic branches from the Germanic regions had their eyes set upon Rome. Julian Nepos was the Emperor of Rome at that time, but was so weak that he was deposed by Orestes within a few months. Orestes was one of Nepos' own military commanders. Instead of assuming the imperial power of the Roman Empire for himself, Orestes appointed his adolescent son, Romulus Augustus, as the new Emperor.

֍

In the year 475, King Odacer controlled a motley group of Germanic vagabonds. Odacer's father was allegedly a Hun and his mother was a member of a small Germanic tribe called the Sciri – which is distantly related to the Goths and Visigoths. They were mostly mercenary soldiers.

֍

King Odacer craved much of the land in Italy and proceeded there with his warriors. He attempted to negotiate with the Roman Emperor in exchange for land in Italy. Orestes, who was the real power behind young Romulus, refused. Odacer then sent out his forces. Of course, the Roman troops were no longer as powerful as they once were and Odacer defeated them. After the battle, Odacer executed Orestes, and called upon Emperor Romulus to appear.

⚜

Romulus greeted him at his tent and handed him a gift – his golden crown. Seeing that this Emperor of Rome was a mere boy of 16, Odacer took pity on him and let him go.

⚜

With neither fanfare nor glory, the last vestiges of the Roman Empire were silently carried into history on the shoulders of a boy. The year was 476 AD.

❧ V ❧

AFTERWORD

❧❧

An angry man is again angry with himself when he returns to reason.

Publilius Syrus

❧❧

Within this book lies the saga of many events both mundane and magnificent. The virtue and depravity of many generations span the centuries from the beginning of the ancient Roman Empire which was once full of vigor and might. Cultures and kingdoms prospered and petered out. Tales about the myths and prophecies concerning Ancient Rome were elucidated here, along with the facts that attest to their truth. The pivotal wars and battles fought for centuries throughout Ancient Rome have been described. Many struggled, lived and died to create the Ancient Roman Empire. They are not unlike us today because their blood courses through our veins and their motivations bear close resemblance to the human spirit we still herald today. The ending of Ancient Rome is sad, as are all endings. You have read and will remember always the last words spoken by the beautiful and tragic woman, Dido of Carthage when you stumble upon the end.

"Rise up my avenging spirit."

And that is what happened when the last light of Ancient Rome vanished like the flame of a candle in the wind.

৩০

YOUR FREE EBOOK!

As a way of saying thank you for reading our book, we're offering you a free copy of the below eBook.

Happy Reading!

GO WWW.THEHISTORYHOUR.COM/CLEO/

Made in the USA
Monee, IL
10 August 2022

11306097R00069